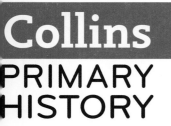

Collins
PRIMARY HISTORY

Ancient Egypt

Pupil Book

Alf Wilkinson

William Collins' dream of knowledge for all began with the publication of his first book in 1819.
A self-educated mill worker, he not only enriched millions of lives, but also founded a flourishing publishing house.
Today, staying true to this spirit, Collins books are packed with inspiration, innovation and practical expertise. They
place you at the centre of a world of possibility and give you exactly what you need to explore it.

Collins. Freedom to teach.

Published by Collins
An imprint of HarperCollins*Publishers*
The News Building
1 London Bridge Street
London
SE1 9GF

HarperCollinsPublishers
1st Floor, Watermarque Building,
Ringsend Road, Dublin 4, Ireland

Browse the complete Collins catalogue at
www.collins.co.uk

© HarperCollins*Publishers* Limited 2019
Maps © Collins Bartholomew 2019

10 9 8 7 6 5 4

ISBN 978-0-00-831083-7

British Library Cataloguing-in-Publication Data
A catalogue record for this publication is available from the British Library.

Author: Alf Wilkinson
Publisher: Lizzie Catford
Product developer: Natasha Paul
Copyeditor: Sally Clifford
Indexer: Jouve India Private Ltd
Proofreader: Nikky Twyman
Image researcher: Alison Prior
Map designer: Gordon MacGilp
Cover designer and illustrator: Steve Evans
Internal designer: EMC Design
Typesetter: Jouve India Private Ltd
Production controller: Rachel Weaver
Printed and bound by Martins the Printers

MIX
Paper from
responsible sources
FSC™ C007454

This book is produced from independently
certified FSC™ paper to ensure responsible
forest management.

For more information visit:
www.harpercollins.co.uk/green

The publishers gratefully acknowledge the permission granted to reproduce the copyright material in this book. Every
effort has been made to trace copyright holders and to obtain their permission for the use of copyright material. The
publishers will gladly receive any information enabling them to rectify any error or omission at the first opportunity.

Contents

'The Egyptian Nile surpasses all rivers of the earth in sweetness of taste, length of course and **utility**. No other river in the world can show such a continuous series of towns and villages along its banks, or a basin so **intensely** cultivated.'

Ibn Battuta

Ibn Battuta, Arab traveller, born 1304 in Morocco

Ibn Battuta wrote those words around 1350 CE, after returning from his travels around the known world. They might have been written in 1350 BCE, or even 2500 BCE. The River Nile, the longest river in the world, is the reason Ancient Egypt existed – without the river, there would have been no Egypt. It is as simple as that!

Water

Most of Egypt is desert. There is not enough rainfall to grow crops or grass for animals to graze. There are raw materials and precious metals in the desert, and limestone for building, but it is very difficult to sustain life without water. People need water to drink, to wash, to fish and to farm. Rivers are important for travel too.

Floods

Every year the River Nile would flood. The winter snow from the mountains in Ethiopia (see Unit 1.2), would melt and the water would arrive in Egypt in July. The river would burst its banks and the land around it would be flooded.

The 'Nilometer' near Cairo. The water would rise up the steps and the column would measure how high the flood was

The Egyptian calendar was split into three seasons:

Flood Season (July–September)

Growing Season (October–February)

Harvest Season (March–June)

After harvest, the **irrigation** canals would be prepared for the next season's flood. There was even a series of 'Nilometers' situated along the Nile in order to measure and **predict** the height of the flood. These were used by rulers to decide how much land would need to be sown after the flood, and also how much to tax the farmers.

The wealth of Egypt depended on the annual flood.

Drought

Sometimes the floods failed. For example, between 2200 BCE and 2150 BCE there were 50 years of low floods. This meant the fields were not as flooded with silt and water each year. Crops would not grow, harvests were much reduced, and there was famine throughout Egypt. We know this because of an inscription on the wall of a tomb in the cemetery of el-Moalla: 'all of Upper Egypt was dying of hunger… everyone had come to eating their children'.

Think about it!

1. The people of Ancient Egypt could predict when the flood would start and how high it would be. Does that mean they were very clever? How do you think they did this?

2. Why is it difficult for people to live in a desert?

3. In what ways was the River Nile important to Egypt?

Let's do it!

1. Find out how the 'Nilometer' worked. Why was this so important to:
   a the rulers of Egypt
   b the farmers of Egypt.

2. Does the River Nile still flood today?

Key words

utility   intensely   irrigation   predict

1.2 Exploring the Nile

The River Nile is the longest river in the world. It is over 6800 kilometres long. The longest branch of the river, the White Nile, starts in the area around Lake Victoria, which sits on the borders of Kenya, Uganda and Tanzania. The branch that supplies most of the water, the Blue Nile, starts in Lake Tana in the highlands of Ethiopia. The two rivers meet near Khartoum, the capital city of Sudan, and then flow north to join the Mediterranean Sea in a huge **delta** around Alexandria.

Finding the source of the Nile

The source of the Nile has been a topic of fascination throughout history. The **cataracts** above Aswan limit shipping. Aswan is the traditional border between Egypt and the Sudan, or Nubia as it was called. In South Sudan there is the Sudd, the largest fresh water swamp in the world, where it is difficult to follow the course of the river. The Roman emperor Nero sent two legions south from Egypt to try to find the source of the Nile. It wasn't until the 15th century that the first European, a Portuguese

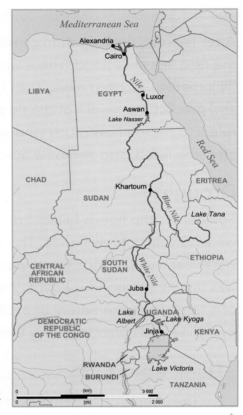

▲ *The River Nile*

European explorers searching for the source of the Nile
▼

monk, reached the source of the Blue Nile, Lake Tana in Ethiopia. Debate continued to rage over the source of the White Nile. It sparked great interest in what was, at the time, called the 'Dark Heart of Africa'.

Many European expeditions set off to try to find the exact source. It wasn't until 1858 that John Hanning Speke, a British army officer, discovered Lake Victoria and declared it was the source of the Nile, although he couldn't really prove it. David Livingstone died trying to find

Inside the library of Alexandria

the source of the Nile. It was 2010 before a definitive source was finally discovered: two tributary rivers that feed into Lake Victoria, in Rwanda and Burundi.

The Aswan Dam

The Aswan Dam, completed in 1970, has completely changed the River Nile. It has created one of the largest man-made lakes in the world, Lake Nasser. It produces hydroelectric power and supplies water for irrigation. But it has stopped the annual flooding, making farming much more difficult for many. It has also reduced the volume of water reaching the Mediterranean Sea.

The Nile Delta

Most Egyptians lived in the narrow strip of 'Black Lands' either side of the River Nile. However, below Cairo, as it approaches the sea, the Nile widens out into a huge delta, of very fertile land. This fertile land is over 250 kilometres wide. At one time there were seven different river channels flowing into the Mediterranean. It was the most intensively farmed area of Egypt. The city of Alexandria is here, founded in the time of Alexander the Great, and today 4.5 million people live there. In the 1st century BCE a Roman visitor said it was 'the first city of the civilised world… in elegance and extent and riches and luxury.' It hosted the biggest library in the world – scholars came from all over to study there. It was a major port and linked the wealth of Egypt with Rome and Greece.

Think about it!

1. Why were people so fascinated by the source of the River Nile?
2. Why was it so difficult to find the source?
3. How did the importance of the River Nile to Egypt change in the 20th century?

Let's do it!

1. Research the Blue Nile and the White Nile. Which contributes most water to the River Nile? Which was the source of the annual floods?
2. Research the 19th-century expeditions to find the source of the Nile. Why did they capture the imagination of people at the time?

Key words

delta
cataracts

1.3 How significant was the River Nile to Egypt?

Egypt at night, taken by satellite from space

Look at the NASA photograph above, taken from space. It shows a modern picture of Egypt at night. Where do nearly all the people of Egypt live? From the photograph, can you work out where the River Nile runs? The electric lights show clearly what the Ancient Egyptians called 'the Black Lands', a strip of land no more than 9 kilometres wide, stretching either side of the River Nile. Can you work out where the Mediterranean Sea is? You can just about make out some of the lights of Southern Europe at the top of the picture.

In this unit we have been studying the River Nile, from its source in Central Africa to the Mediterranean Sea, and from ancient times right up to today.

If something is very important, historians talk about it being significant. Historians have special **criteria,** or reasons, to help them decide whether someone or something is significant.

Deciding if something is/was significant

Ian Dawson, a well-known historian and history teacher, uses these criteria for deciding significance.

Something is significant if it:

- changed events at the time.
- improved lots of people's lives – or made them worse.
- changed people's ideas.
- had a long-lasting impact on the country or the world.
- had been a really good or a very bad example to other people of how to live or behave.

So, using these criteria, do you think the River Nile was significant for Egypt? And do you think it is still significant today? Significance can vary from time to time.

The River Nile in Egypt in modern times

Key word

criteria

Think about it!

1. Do you agree with Ian Dawson's criteria for deciding whether something is significant?
2. Can you come up with criteria of your own?

Let's do it!

1. Make a list of all the things the Egyptians used the River Nile for.
2. Make a list of all the things in Egypt that would not have happened without the River Nile.
3. Decide just how significant the River Nile:
   a was to life in Egypt in ancient times
   b is to life in Egypt today.

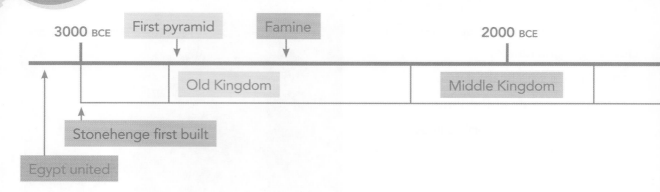

People settled in the Nile Valley around about 5000 BCE, but most historians agree that Egypt became a united country around 3100 BCE, when Upper Egypt and Lower Egypt were united by King Narmer. Around this time, **hieroglyphics** are first used to write things down – perhaps that is why we regard it as the first civilisation of Egypt.

The Old Kingdom

The Old Kingdom emerged under King Djoser about 2682 BCE. Early Egyptian rulers were known as kings rather than pharaohs. Imhotep, a leading official of Djoser, is said to have designed and built the first pyramid – a step pyramid – in 2667 BCE. It was a time of peace and prosperity, and the building of temples and palaces. The Great Pyramid of Giza (the biggest building in the whole world until Lincoln Cathedral was built in the Middle Ages) and the Sphinx were built by Khufu around 2558 BCE. It is at this time that the ruler became a god, and was worshipped because he was the one who could control the floods of the Nile. The population rose to around 3 million people. Towards the end of the period, weak rulers and famine led to civil wars and the end of the Old Kingdom.

King Djoser's pyramid at Saqqara, finished around 2650 BCE

The Middle Kingdom

Mentuhotep II reunited Egypt around 2055 BCE, bringing together all the separate kingdoms. Sinai and Nubia were reconquered, and the Nile floods were good, so agriculture prospered. The pharaohs became powerful again, carefully controlling government and taxes. For the first time there was a full-time army defending Egypt. Trading expeditions were sent out across the Middle East, bringing wealth to the country.

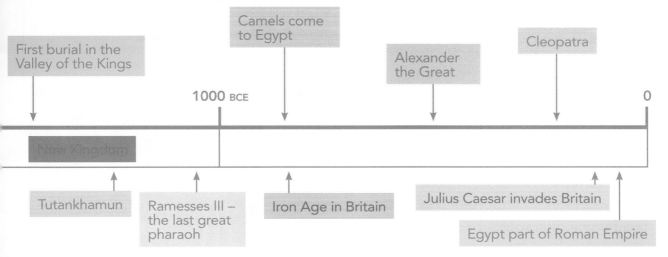

First burial in the Valley of the Kings

Camels come to Egypt

Alexander the Great

Cleopatra

1000 BCE

0

New Kingdom

Tutankhamun

Ramesses III – the last great pharaoh

Iron Age in Britain

Julius Caesar invades Britain

Egypt part of Roman Empire

The New Kingdom

This is the period when Egypt was at its greatest, conquering many neighbouring territories. It controlled much of what we now know as the Middle East, as well as further up the River Nile. Pharaohs were no longer buried in pyramids, but were buried in tombs in the Valley of the Kings, on the West Bank of the River Nile. This is the time of Hatshepsut, the great female pharaoh, Tutankhamun and Nefertiti, and Ramesses III. After Ramesses died, weaker rulers failed to hold together the Egyptian Empire and it once again split into several parts.

▲ *Statue of Mentuhotep II*

Decline and fall

Egypt became more and more open to invasion from outside. The Persians conquered Egypt in 525 BCE and then Alexander the Great conquered it in 332 BCE. Finally, under Cleopatra, Egypt became part of the Roman Empire around 30 BCE, supplying Rome with food shipped across the Mediterranean Sea.

Think about it!

1. When do you think Egypt was at its most powerful?
2. Which do you think was more important for making Egypt powerful: a strong ruler or the floods of the River Nile?

Let's do it!

1. Find out about Egyptian step pyramids. How are they similar, and how are they different, to other pyramids?
2. How useful is the statue of Mentuhotep II in telling us:
   a what he looked like?
   b what he achieved?
   c what people at the time thought of him?

Key word

hieroglyphics

Throughout the whole period of Ancient Egypt, the country was ruled by a pharaoh. Before the time of the New Kingdom, they had a variety of titles such as 'Lord of the Two Lands' and 'High Priest of Every Temple'. These titles give us a clue as to why a pharaoh was so important. He – there were very few female pharaohs – had total power and control over the country. This meant that it was important that the pharaoh was a strong leader. Usually, when a pharaoh died, his son would become the next pharaoh.

Controller of everyday life

The pharaoh owned all the land in Egypt. It all belonged to him. He set the level of taxes to be paid – everyone had to pay the cost of building pyramids and temples – and decided which laws would be passed. His seal was needed on every official document, to prove what he wanted done. He would hold **audiences** every day, where people could ask him to solve disputes, to grant favours or for promotion to new jobs.

The symbols of kingship in Ancient Egypt – a flail and a crook. The crook, a tool of shepherds, shows that the pharaoh leads and protects his people. The flail symbolises the pharaoh's role as the provider of food for his people

Nemes head cloth usually worn by a pharaoh, with cobra and vulture heads ▶

Defender of the country

When the country was threatened, it was the pharaoh's job to lead the army into battle, although sometimes he would send his generals in his place, especially if the war was a long way from the capital. We have already seen that a weak pharaoh could lead to Egypt falling apart.

Religion

The Egyptians treated the pharaoh as a god. He was Horus, the son of Ra, the Sun God. He was also responsible for making sure all the other gods were kept happy, by making offerings and sacrifices in the temple. It was his job to make sure the Nile floods came each year, to keep the country wealthy.

The pharaoh was a god as well as ruler of Egypt.

Think about it!

1. Which of the roles of a pharaoh do you think was most important? Why?

2. Why do you think there were so few female pharaohs?

Key word

audiences

Let's do it!

1. Hatshepsut, 1473–1458 BCE, and Cleopatra, 51–30 BCE, were two famous female pharaohs. Can you find any more?

2. Split into groups and research a pharaoh. Why were they important? Did they carry out all the functions of a pharaoh? Feed back to the class.

3. Were all pharaohs the same? In what ways were they different?

Giving the pharaoh gifts

One of the best ways to really get to know about Ancient Egypt is to develop a sense of what was it really like to live at that time – or, in this case, what was it like to be the pharaoh for the day.

Surrounded by officials and servants

From the moment he woke up to the moment he went to bed, the pharaoh would be surrounded by people, responding to his every wish and need. There would be servants to deal with washing, dressing and appearance; there would be officials to deal with business – the **Vizier**, Scribes, the Chief Treasurer, the Controller of the State Granaries – there would be the general of armies to talk with; priests and noble men and women, even a Royal Sandal Bearer and Royal Fan Bearer. Everything would be organised for him. There would also be family – many pharaohs

Many pharaohs had several wives and lots of children.

had several wives and lots of children – and friends, and perhaps the Queen Mother, wife of a previous pharaoh. There might even be officials from other countries to meet and talk to. All these people would be jostling for attention and making demands on the pharaoh's time.

Akhenaten 1350–1334 BCE – A typical pharaoh?

Akhenaten changed religion in Egypt. Instead of many gods, he believed in one deity, Aten, and insisted that everyone else abandon the old ways and worship the Aten too. He built huge temples to Aten. He even

▲ *Akhenaten shown as a sphinx, with rays from the sun (the usual way the god Aten was shown) bathing him in light and power*

built a new royal city, Akhetaten, away from any existing religious temples and influences, which was home to 50,000 people. New styles of architecture and art were introduced. But it was all too much change for the people of Egypt. When his son, Tutankhamun, became pharaoh, he returned to the old ways. Akhetaten was discredited, the new temples to Aten were deserted, and the old temples restored and rebuilt. Many of Akhenaten's monuments and statues were defaced and destroyed and his name was removed from the list of Egypt's rulers. It wasn't until the 20th century that archaeologists began to discover his works and ideas.

Key word

Vizier

Think about it!

1. How much time do you think the pharaoh would have to himself?
2. If the pharaoh himself didn't make decisions, who would?
3. How would the government of Egypt work without the pharaoh?
4. Was Akhenaten a typical pharaoh?

Let's do it!

1. Find out what each of the people surrounding the pharaoh did. Which of them do you think were most important? Which would have greatest access to the pharaoh? Who would have influence and power?
2. Imagine you are the Royal Diary Keeper. Draw up a timetable for the pharaoh for a day. How much time would you allocate to each person trying to see him?

Most Egyptians were farmers – their lives were driven by the three seasons. As the Nile's floods went down, they planted their crops. They grew wheat for bread, flax for clothes, papyrus for writing on and fruit and vegetables to eat. Bees were kept for honey to sweeten foods. Geese and ducks provided eggs, and cattle gave milk. There were fish in the river, and wild animals and wild birds to hunt for food. Some of the crops were paid as taxes to the priests and the pharaoh. As Ancient Egyptians didn't have money, they used a system of **barter** – exchanging goods for something else that you wanted.

Ploughing using cattle; a picture on the wall of a burial chamber, c1200 BCE

Egyptian farmers trained monkeys to climb up high trees and pick fruit and throw it down!

Craftsmen

Not everyone was a farmer – there were plenty of other jobs to be done too. Craftsmen might make pots or jewellery; weapons or boats; cloth, leather sandals or bread, mud bricks for building, or any of the other goods that were needed. Some would be soldiers or sailors, some water-carriers, and others worked as scribes writing letters and keeping accounts. Some mined gold in the desert or cut stone for new buildings. Sons tended to follow their fathers, being trained into and then doing the same job. The surplus food grown meant that there was plenty to feed those families living in the towns and cities, and even lots left over to sell to other countries.

Houses

Ordinary people's houses were very simple. They needed to be built away from the river, above the flood levels. Sometimes built on stone foundations, they were made of dried mud, and painted white, to reflect the heat of the sun. The windows were small – there was no glass – and rooms were dark. There might be only two or three rooms. Some houses had a cellar underground for storing food. Grain needed to be ground and bread needed to be baked every day. Most people did their cooking outside over an open fire. Most meals for ordinary people were based on bread. In the summer, people would sleep on the roof to try to keep cool at night. Egyptians slept on hard wooden beds, and instead of a pillow they had a wooden headrest.

Harvest time

Picking grapes

Think about it!

1. Do you think life was hard for Egyptian farmers?

2. If you lived in Ancient Egypt, would you rather be a craftsman or a farmer? Why?

3. Make a list of the ways an Egyptian farmer's house is similar to, and different from, your own house. Which would you rather live in? Why?

Let's do it!

1. Find out which crops Egyptian farmers grew. Some have been mentioned here, but there were plenty of others.

2. Find out which animals, fish and birds the Ancient Egyptians hunted for food.

3. Why do you think scenes (like the ones shown in the images on this page) were painted on the walls of tombs belonging to rich Egyptians?

Key word

barter

In 1922, French **archaeologists** stumbled across the remains of the village of Deir el-Medina, on the west bank of the River Nile, near Luxor. Over the next 30 years, the village was **excavated** and lots was discovered about the lives of the people who lived there. It is quite unusual to find out so much about how ordinary people lived and worked. The village was near the Valley of the Kings, where rich Egyptians and pharaohs were buried in the time of the New Kingdom. It was a walled village, used from c1500 BCE until around 1100 BCE. There were 68 houses in total, along each side of a main street.

The remains of the workmen's village of Deir el-Medina

The village

The village of Deir el-Medina tells us lots about the lives of the ordinary people of Ancient Egypt.

The village was in the desert, 2 miles from the River Nile, with no water, so it was not a farming village. In fact, the inhabitants were all skilled craftsmen, employed by the pharaoh, to work on tombs and monuments. They included stone-cutters, carpenters, plasterers and water-carriers. Unusually, it is estimated that 40 per cent of the population of Deir el-Medina could read and write, whereas the average for the whole of Ancient Egypt at the time was only 1 per cent! Many personal letters have been discovered that tell us a great deal about everyday life.

Many of the craftsmen were quite well off. They had servants to do the chores – grinding grain, doing the laundry, fetching water from the River Nile. They would work eight days, then have two days off. They were paid in rations, and would receive extra food, salt, even meat, on special occasions and festivals. In their spare time, they went hunting and fishing, played board games and held wrestling contests. Women would care for the children and bake the bread. Often the women would receive a note from their husband or son to bring them something up to the workplace – a new trowel, or clean clothes, or some food. This is how we know so much about their lives – there is plenty of written evidence.

Houses

Houses were long and narrow. Many had only three or four rooms. Many rooms had **niches** in the wall for an icon or model of the family's family god. Some families had converted the front room into a shop, where people would sell or barter items they had made – jewellery, sandals, lamps, etc – with other workers. Some families lived in the same houses in the village, doing the same jobs, for several hundred years.

A painting of an Ancient Egyptian house

Decorating a shrine in a tomb at Luxor. Carpenters at work

Key words

archaeologists
excavated
niches

Think about it!

1. Do you think evidence of the lives of ordinary people is useful?
2. Which do you think is more useful – the archaeological evidence or the written evidence found at Deir el-Medina?

Let's do it!

1. Compare the artist's painting of a house with what you have discovered in Units 3.1 and 3.2. How useful is the painting to historians?
2. Find out about other UNESCO sites in Egypt. Are they similar to Deir el-Medina?
3. Which piece of evidence tells us the most about life in Ancient Egypt – a modern photograph, an artist's painting, or a scene from a tomb made during the New Kingdom? Why?

'I will make you love writing more than
   your mother,
I will show its beauties to you;
Now, it is greater than any trade,
There is not one like it in the land.

I have seen the metal-worker working
At the mouth of his furnace;
With fingers like the stuff of a crocodile
He stinks more than fish eggs.

The carpenter who uses an **adze**,
He is more tired than a worker in the fields;
His field is the wood, his hoe the adze.
His work is endless...

The jeweller drills with his chisel
In different kinds of stone;
Once he is done with the inlay of the eyes
His arms are weary, he is tired;
Sitting down at sunset,
His knees and back ache.

The barber is still shaving at the end of
   the day,
To the town he takes himself,
To his corner he takes himself,
From street to street he takes himself
To search for people to shave.
He works with his arms to fill his belly,
Like a bee which can only eat as it has worked.

Look, no trade is free from a director,
Except the scribe's: he is the director.
But if you know writings, it will be better for you,
More than these trades I have shown you.'

In a society where only 1 per cent of people could read and write, scribes were very important people!

Think about it!

1. How useful is this text in telling us about the lives of craftsmen in Ancient Egypt?

2. Do you think Duaf is accurately describing the life of each craftsman, or is he biased in favour of scribes? How can you tell?

Let's do it!

1. Find out about both the training and the work of scribes. How difficult was it to become a scribe, and how important were they in Ancient Egyptian life?

Key word

adze

Painting, by Herbert M. Herget, showing a rich person's house
▼

The houses of rich people were much grander, often built around a pool of water to help keep the home cool, and there would be plenty of servants and slaves to do all the hard work. There were high walls around the house to keep out unwanted visitors.

Wood was expensive. Egyptian trees were not very good for making furniture, so timber was imported from Byblos – in present-day Lebanon. Furniture made of imported wood was only found in the homes of the rich. Rich people displayed precious items in their homes: rugs from Persia, ebony and ivory from the Upper Nile region, golden vases, jewellery from Nubia, precious stones and gold ornaments.

Think about it!

1. Look carefully at this painting. What can you discover about the homes of the rich from the painting?
2. In what ways were the houses of rich people similar to the houses of ordinary people in Ancient Egypt? In what ways were they different?
3. How useful is this painting in telling us about rich people's houses?
4. Would you rather live in a rich person's home or an ordinary person's home? Why?

Let's do it!

1. What have you already discovered about everyday life in Ancient Egypt?
2. As a class, make a list of questions you still want to ask about everyday life in Ancient Egypt. Where might you find the answers to these questions?
3. Which is the best piece of evidence you have come across about everyday life in Ancient Egypt? Why?

Women and children

Family was very important to the Ancient Egyptians. Men would marry around the age of 20, and women at 14 years old. Rich men might have several wives, but most men only had one. Poor women would spend their days cooking and cleaning, looking after the children, and helping their husband work on the family farm or business. Better-off women would have slaves or servants to do the hard work for them, which meant that they were free to run their own businesses. Divorce was easy if a woman was **mistreated** by her husband – all she had to do was say she wanted a divorce in front of witnesses.

Clothes

Clothes were light and simple, because of the heat. Most were made of linen, from flax grown in the fields. The youngest stems of flax made the finest linen, which was almost see-through. Spinning and weaving were important jobs for many women. Cloth would be bleached in the sun to make it whiter, although natural dyes were used to make bright colours.

Women wearing simple white linen dresses, from a tomb painting

Musicians, from a tomb painting

Jobs

Many women stayed at home – one phrase used to describe a woman was 'the lady of the house'. But women could work, and many did. They worked as musicians, acrobats, singers and dancers; they could be priestesses in the temple; they might be weavers, gardeners or even doctors or record-keepers. They could own their own property, run their own businesses and often, when their husband was away, run their husband's business too.

Although women in Ancient Egypt were not equal with men, they had many rights.

Adapted from *Ancient History for Kids*

Harvesting wheat, from a tomb painting

'Egyptian women had a free life, compared to her contemporaries in other lands. She wasn't a **feminist**, but she could have power and position if she was in the right class. She could hold down a job, or be a mother if she chose. She could live by herself or with her family. She could buy and sell to her heart's content. She could follow the latest fashions or learn to write if she had the chance... She helped her husband, she ran her household. She lived a similar life to that of her mother and grandmother... She was an ancient Egyptian woman with hopes and dreams of her own... not too much different from woman of today.'

Caroline Seawright, *Women in Ancient Egypt*

Key words

mistreated
feminist
gender

Think about it!

1. How do the two interpretations on this page agree on what life was like for women in Ancient Egypt?

2. Do they give a complete picture? What else would you like to know about life for women in Ancient Egypt?

3. Was life good for women in Ancient Egypt? Why do you think this?

Let's do it!

1. Egyptians loved makeup. Find out what women – and men – used for makeup, and how it looked.

2. Research the jobs women did – some are mentioned here, but you will find others. Did the status of women depend on their **gender**, or on their wealth?

> *'Today is the happiest day of my life –
> we have finally adopted a child.'*
> Egyptian woman, writing in 1875 BCE

A toy cat with pull-along string

Caring for children

Ancient Egyptians loved children, and often had large families. Many babies died from infection and disease – some historians suggest more than one in three babies died. To help counteract this, mothers would breastfeed their children until they were three years old, and then wean them onto vegetables and a **gruel** or porridge made from stewed wheat or barley sweetened with honey or dates.

Children would wear no clothes until they were around 10 years old, making it easier to keep clean. They would have all their hair shaved off, apart from one long plait, or side-lock, that hung down one side of their head. Shaving off the side-lock was a sign that they were now an adult.

A doll made of wood, with hair made from clay beads

Fun and games

Much of life would be spent outside, playing. Everyone would learn to swim, but also to be careful of the crocodiles and hippopotamuses in the River Nile. Boys would learn to fight with sticks, spears and bows and arrows so they could hunt and fish or fight in the army of the pharaoh when they were older. Girls would learn to grind corn, cook, spin and weave and generally look after the household. But there were plenty of games too – many we still recognise today. Leapfrog and tug-of-war were popular, as were spinning tops, ball games, dolls and pull-along toys. Board games were very popular, the two best known were called Snake and Senet.

Pets were very popular. Many Egyptian families would have cats or dogs, birds or even monkeys as household pets, but these animals would be expected to earn their keep too. Cats would kill rats and mice in the granary; dogs would help with hunting; and monkeys were trained to climb tall trees and pick fruit and pass it down to people waiting below.

Jobs and careers

Children were expected to obey their parents without question, and were expected to help around the house from an early age. One Egyptian word for 'child' translates as 'servant', and another describes boys as 'walking sticks for their fathers'. Boys were expected to learn their father's trade and follow in his footsteps.

◀ *Boy milking cow, from a wall painting in Saqqara*

Key word

gruel

Think about it!

1. Why might adopting a child make this woman so happy? What does that tell us about attitudes towards children in Ancient Egypt?
2. Do you think it was fun being a child in Ancient Egypt?
3. How different was life for rich and poor children?

Let's do it!

1. Find out how you play Snake and/or Senet. Describe the rules to others in your group.
2. Write a story about a day, or an event, in the life of a young Egyptian boy or girl. Remember to make it realistic. Use examples from this unit, or that you have discovered for yourself.

Going to school

Only rich boys went to school – very few Egyptians could read and write. They would be taught by a priest in the temple. They would learn reading and writing as well as mathematics. Some girls would learn to read and write – when their husband was away, they would be expected to run the household and the family business. Writing was complicated to learn, as there were over 1000 different hieroglyphs used. Girls would usually be taught at home by their mothers. They would learn the skills they would normally need in their daily life.

▲
Writing in Ancient Egypt

Diversity

You will have noticed, as you have worked through this unit, that life in Ancient Egypt was very different for the rich and for the poor. Rich people had servants and slaves to look after them, much nicer and bigger houses, and ate better foods. You will also have probably noticed that there were differences between the lives of men and women, and between boys and girls. There were also big differences between living in the countryside as a farmer or labourer and living in the towns and cities as a craftsman or noble. This reminds us about diversity – that not everyone is, or was, the same. When we talk about life in Ancient Egypt, we have to be very careful to make clear who we are talking about.

> *'Diversity' means 'difference' – not everyone in Egypt was the same.*

We also need to think about how similar, and how different, life in Ancient Egypt was from life today. For example, did women in Ancient Egypt have more or less equality than women today? You might decide to compare the lives of women in Ancient Egypt with women in another period of history you may have already studied, like in Ancient Greece or Anglo-Saxon times.

Think about it!

1. Caroline Seawright, in 'Women in Ancient Egypt', argues that women were 'not too much different from woman of today'. Do you agree?
2. Would you rather have grown up in Ancient Egypt or today? Why?

Let's do it!

1. What were the main differences between growing up rich and growing up poor in Ancient Egypt?
2. Make a list of all the jobs women do today. How similar is your list to the list of what women did in Ancient Egypt?
3. In what ways was going to school in Ancient Egypt similar to going to school today? In what ways is it different?
4. Draw up a table showing ways that growing up in Ancient Egypt was similar to growing up today, and ways that it is different.

Were all Egyptians buried in pyramids?

Egyptians believed that you needed your body after death. To **preserve** the body, they **mummified** it. This was a long and expensive process, taking around 70 days to complete. The body was washed and cleaned, and the organs, except for the heart, were removed. The body was then filled with stuffing and dried by covering it with a substance called natron, a natural salt. This absorbed all the moisture from the body. After 40–50 days, the stuffing was removed and replaced with linen or sawdust. The body was wrapped in strands of linen and covered in a sheet called a shroud. Finally, the body was placed in a stone coffin called a sarcophagus.

Egyptian mummy and case on display in the British Museum, London

Ma'at is the Ancient Egyptian goddess of truth. When you died, your heart was weighed against Ma'at's feather. You were only admitted to the **afterlife** if your heart was lighter than the feather. When you died, your heart was left in your body.

Canopic jars

Each of the major organs of the body (liver, intestines, lungs and stomach) was placed in its own canopic jar. Each jar was decorated with the head of one of the sons of the god Horus. The canopic jars were placed in the tomb with the mummified remains.

Canopic jars on display in the Michael C. Carlos Museum in Georgia, USA

Pyramids

As we have already discovered in Units 2.1 and 2.2, during the Old and Middle Kingdoms rich and powerful Egyptians were buried in pyramids. The biggest was at Giza, built in 2589 BCE for Khufu, and was nearly 150 metres tall. It is made from over 2.3 million blocks of limestone, some of which weigh 15 tons. Originally the outside was covered with a layer of brilliant white limestone, although this was later taken away to be used in the city of Cairo. Thousands of labourers and craftsmen were needed to build a pyramid. Special villages, like Deir el-Medina (which we looked at in Unit 3.2) were built nearby to house the craftsmen. Labourers worked on pyramids during the flood season.

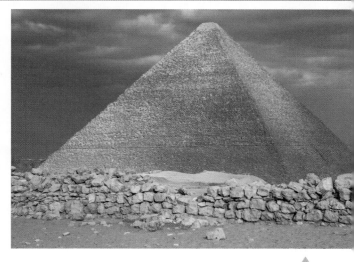

The Great Pyramid of Giza

Almost as soon as he became ruler of Egypt, a pharaoh would plan and build his pyramid. Pyramids were designed to protect the body of the pharaoh after his death. There were false passages and tightly fitting doors. There were even spells written on the walls, to deter tomb robbers who were searching for all the wealth buried with the pharaoh. After all, a pharaoh would need all his riches in the afterlife. Unfortunately, tomb robbers managed to raid virtually every pyramid and steal the treasures.

Key words

preserve
mummified
afterlife

Think about it!

1. Why were rich Egyptians turned into mummies?
2. How do tombs help us to understand life in Ancient Egypt, even if the contents have been stolen?
3. Why was the design of the insides of many pyramids so complicated?

Let's do it!

1. Read the story *Ma'at's Feather* by Juliet Desailly. Qen is tricked by his older brother into raiding a tomb. Qen gets caught and is punished for his part in the tomb raid.
2. Find out how the pyramids were built.
3. Why did Egyptians stop building pyramids in about 1700 BCE?

How secure were tombs in the Valley of the Kings?

For over 500 years during the New Kingdom, pharaohs and important people were buried in the **necropolis** in the Valley of the Kings. Over 60 tombs have been discovered in the Valley of the Kings. Only around 20 of them belong to pharaohs – the rest are those of pharaohs' wives and royal officials. Historians suggest the isolated, hot and dry valley was chosen as a burial ground because it was remote and uninhabited, which would be to deter grave-robbers. Special armed guards were stationed at the entrance of the valley to protect the tombs. Unfortunately, all but one were robbed, probably before 1000 BCE.

Map showing the pyramids and the Valley of the Kings

Tombs contained all the valuable items you would associate with a pharaoh or a noble, but also the everyday items needed in the afterlife – food and drink, furniture, combs, clothes and jewellery were all included. Even pets were buried alongside their owner. The walls were decorated with sacred texts, as well as scenes from everyday life. Tombs vary in size – from a simple one-room burial in a cleft in the hill, to elaborate tombs with over 100 different rooms, dug deep down into the rock. Ways into the tombs were carefully hidden. The Valley of the Kings has been a major focus for archaeological investigation over the last 200 years.

What if you couldn't afford to be mummified?

Ordinary people were not so lucky. They would be buried in the desert, in a shallow grave, wrapped in a reed blanket and covered with stones, to protect them from wild animals. The dry desert air would gradually mummify the remains, and from time to time these bodies are discovered. Simple grave goods – usually food and drink for the afterlife – were placed in the grave. It was all that most people could afford.

Aerial view of the Valley of the Kings, near Luxor, on the West Bank of the Nile

Key word

necropolis

Think about it!

1. Why do you think all these pharaohs were buried in the Valley of the Kings rather than in pyramids?

2. What measures did tomb builders take to try to prevent tomb robberies?

3. In what ways were burials of rich and poor people in Ancient Egypt similar? In what ways were they different?

Inside the tomb of Ramesses IV today

Tomb of an unknown craftsman, Deir el-Medina

Let's do it!

1. Research the goods that were buried with Tutankhamun. Why have they caused such a sensation, wherever they have been displayed around the world?

2. Near the Valley of the Kings was the Valley of the Queens. Find out about the Valley of the Queens. Why did they stop burying royal women in the Valley of the Kings and start to bury them in the Valley of the Queens?

Tutankhamun

The one tomb from the Valley of the Kings that was not robbed was that of Tutankhamun. This was discovered by English archaeologist Howard Carter in 1922. What was so special about his tomb that protected it from robbery? Tutankhamun was buried in three coffin cases of gold, and these were placed inside a stone sarcophagus. Alongside these was a dagger made of iron – a rare and precious metal at the time, worth much more than the golden dagger that lay beside it! Altogether, over 3000 items were found in the tomb of the 18-year-old pharaoh, giving us a fascinating insight into the life of a pharaoh in the New Kingdom. These are now on display in the Egyptian Museum in Cairo.

The entrance to Tutankhamun's tomb in the Valley of the Kings today

Continuity and change

One important skill in history is to be able to see when things have stayed the same and when things have changed. Ancient Egypt lasted for over 3000 years, from c3100 BCE to around 30 BCE. Therefore, some things must have changed over that much time, but many stayed the same. Pictures of pharaohs and everyday life from tomb walls remain very similar throughout the whole period of Egyptian history. Yet there was political change, as we have discovered. The Old Kingdom disintegrated and split up, before being reunited as the Middle Kingdom. This also split up, before the New Kingdom emerged stronger than ever. However, throughout it all, life depended on the annual floods of the River Nile.

A funeral procession, from the Book of the Dead

Think about it!

1. Think about the way pharaohs were buried. How did this change between the Old Kingdom and the New Kingdom?
2. Is there one period where things changed more quickly?
3. Are there any aspects of the burial of pharaohs that stayed the same?
4. Pharaohs were gods, so their tombs were temples. Would you have raided a tomb for what was inside it?

Let's do it!

1. Find out about the god Osiris and the Egyptian idea of the afterlife.
2. Why did Egyptians feel they needed to be buried with grave goods?
3. Which is more important over the whole of Ancient Egypt: continuity in the way people were buried, or change? Why?

The River Nile was the motorway of Ancient Egypt, and wherever possible travel was by river. Every city, town and village was next to the river. In the flood season, it was easy to sail down the river towards the coast. In the dry season, the wind was from north to south, making it easier to use sails to work your way up the river away from the coast.

▲ *Fishing on the Nile using a boat made out of papyrus*

River boats

Smaller boats were made from bundles of **papyrus** tied together. They had a very distinctive pointed front, which helped them to float. These boats were used for short distances, as ferries to cross the river or for fishing.

Wooden boats

Larger boats were made of timber. The best boats were made of cedar wood that was imported from Lebanon. Sails and oars were used to power the boat, and one (or sometimes two) rear steering oars were used to guide the boat. We know about these boats because many models have been found in tombs. In 1991 at Abydos, archaeologists found the remains of 14 boats dating back to around 2900 BCE buried in the sand. These helped them to work out just how boats were built.

Trade

Egypt exported papyrus, grain, linen, ox hides, lentils and dried fish. It imported goods from around the Red Sea and throughout the Mediterranean. Perfume and pottery came from Greece. Pine and cedar wood, copper sheets, amber, amethyst and ostrich eggs were brought from Lebanon. Semi-precious stones like turquoise and malachite came from Sinai. Ebony, ivory and gold came from Nubia. Galena, from the Red Sea coast, was used to make the black eye makeup that both men and women loved so much.

Hatshepsut and Puntland

Around 1470 BCE, Hatshepsut, the female pharaoh, sent an expedition to Puntland, which was known as a region rich in resources. Historians think it was the area that we now know as Somalia and Yemen. Boats were taken to pieces and carried across the desert to the Red Sea. From there, they sailed for Puntland. The expedition traded for incense, gold, ivory, leopardskins, pottery, ostrich feathers and myrrh, which was used to make both incense and fragrant oils. Living myrrh trees were carefully planted in barrels of soil and brought back to Egypt. The expedition was seen as a great success.

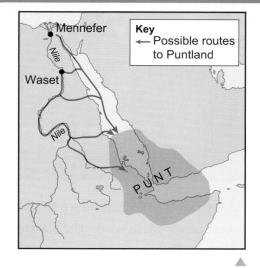

Map showing the possible location of Puntland

Historians are still not sure exactly where Puntland was.

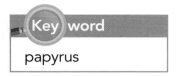

Key word

papyrus

Think about it!

1. How significant was the River Nile as a transport route? Which time of year was best for travel?

2. What kind of goods did Hatshepsut's expedition bring back from Puntland? Were they for rich people or ordinary people?

3. What kind of goods did Egypt export? Were they for rich people or ordinary people?

Let's do it!

1. Make a 'trade map' for Ancient Egypt, showing all the places mentioned in the text that Egypt bought and sold goods with.

2. Find out about the boats excavated at Abydos in 1991. How big were they? How were they made? What were they used for? How similar, and how different were they to the boat in the picture?

3. How important was trade to Ancient Egypt?

As well as training, soldiers might be given other work when they were not fighting. They might be employed to move stone for new buildings, to work as policemen or to carry messages. A soldier could be expected to march 20 kilometres a day and then build a camp surrounded by a wall of shields before settling down for the night. An army might have 12,000 foot soldiers and 3000 charioteers. The pharaoh would be expected to lead it into battle.

Wooden figures of soldiers, from around 2000 BCE

Weapons used by Egyptian soldiers. Can you work out what they are and what they are made from? Which period are they from?

Weapons

Weapons used by the army changed from flint in the Old Kingdom, to bronze in the Middle Kingdom and iron in the New Kingdom. However, iron was expensive and difficult to make, as wood was needed to melt the iron ore and Egypt was short of trees. At the same time, stronger and improved bows with a longer range were developed. Finally, in the New Kingdom, Egypt had a full-time, well-trained army. By this time, soldiers might have worn chain mail.

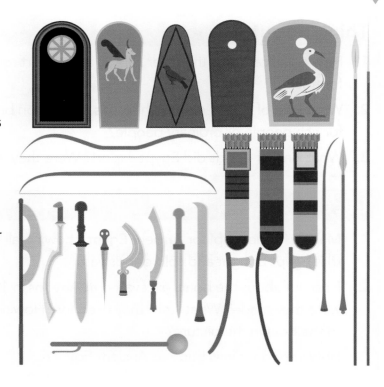

At war

In battle, experienced soldiers fought in the frontline, with new recruits close behind. The chariots would try to break through enemy lines and then the infantry would charge in to finish off the enemy. Quite often, the battle would be a siege, trying to capture a town or city protected by strong walls. If a soldier was injured, army doctors would treat him (see Unit 7.2 for more on medicine). Generals prided themselves on losing very few of their soldiers, so tried hard not to lose men unnecessarily. Pharaohs would hire professional soldiers from other countries (**mercenaries**), like Nubia and even Greece, to strengthen their armies.

▲ *Fighting in a chariot. Chariots were introduced to Egypt in the Middle Kingdom*

Changes in weapons and tactics were usually a result of war with other countries. For example, the horse and war chariot was introduced following the conflict with invaders from the region of Syria. Later, iron weapons were developed following war with the Hittites. It was during the New Kingdom that Egypt's armies were at their most feared. Perhaps their most famous victory was around 1178 BCE, when Ramesses III defeated the invasion by the Sea Peoples and the Libyans in a combined land and sea battle.

Think about it!

1. Why might someone join the army today? Was it the same in Ancient Egypt?
2. What would it have been like being a soldier in Ancient Egypt? Would you rather have been an infantryman, an archer or a charioteer? Why?

Let's do it!

1. Investigate the weapons and tactics used by Egypt, and how they changed between the Old Kingdom and the New Kingdom. Which were most effective?
2. Find out about Egypt's navy. How successful was it?
3. If the army was so strong, why did the Old Kingdom, the Middle Kingdom and the New Kingdom all end in fighting?
4. How does the army of Ancient Egypt compare with other armies you have studied – for example, the Roman army?

Key word

mercenaries

How inventive were the Ancient Egyptians?

We have already seen that the Ancient Egyptians moved huge blocks of stone to build the pyramids. They discovered that if you poured water onto the sand in front of the blocks of stone, it was much easier to drag the stones on their sledge into place. If possible, limestone blocks were quarried close to where the pyramid was to be, or transported there by river.

Irrigation

The Nile floods might raise the river level by up to 15 metres, depositing silt on the fields. But, once the floods went down, how were the crops in the fields watered? The Egyptians built earth walls around their fields to collect the water and stop it draining away. They also built a series of irrigation channels, where water was carefully diverted into each field in turn. Channels were carefully built on a slope so the water ran downhill, but slowly enough to prevent erosion of the land. They also invented a very simple way to raise water by hand. This was the shaduf. If the fields were too far away from the river, then water had to be carried to them in big earthenware jars.

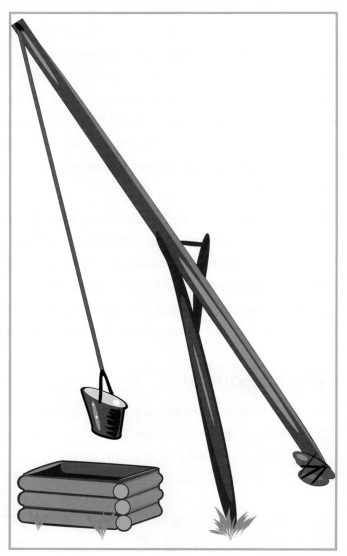

A drawing of a shaduf

Irrigation was very important to Egyptian farmers.

Telling the time

By around 2500 BCE, the Egyptians had developed a calendar of 12 months made up of 30 days. Five 'extra' days were added at the end of the year to make 365 days. This was based on the movement of the stars in the sky. We have already seen (Unit 1.1) that the year was split into three seasons.

Days were split into 24 hours – 12 of daylight and 12 of night. *An Egyptian water clock*
At first, shadow clocks and sundials were used to tell the time in daylight. Later, from around 1400 BCE, water clocks were used. These worked by measuring the amount of water that flowed through the clock, and markers on the side of the container showed the hour.

Other inventions

The Egyptians invented both the sickle and the ox-drawn plough, making farming much easier. They also invented a kind of paper to write on, made from the inside of the stems of the papyrus reed which grew widely in the Nile Delta. Because it could not be easily folded, sheets of papyrus were made into **scrolls**. Short documents were easy to carry around, but a book needed a very long scroll. They also developed a number system that allowed them to carry out very complicated calculations.

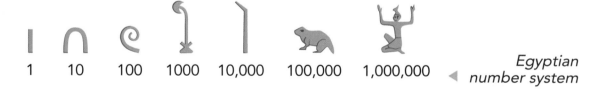

| 1 | 10 | 100 | 1000 | 10,000 | 100,000 | 1,000,000 |

◄ *Egyptian number system*

Think about it!

1. Look closely at the picture of a shaduf. Can you figure out how it worked? It is very simple. Does that mean the Ancient Egyptians weren't very inventive?

2. Why was it so important that Ancient Egyptians could tell the time?

Let's do it!

1. Find out how the Ancient Egyptians lifted those huge blocks of stone when building a pyramid.

2. Try doing some maths using the Egyptian symbols for numbers. Make up 10 calculations for a friend to complete.

3. Make either a shadow clock/ sundial or a water clock. In what ways is your clock similar to one used by the Ancient Egyptians? In what ways is it different?

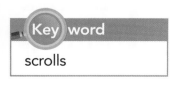

Key word

scrolls

'In Egypt, the men are more skilled in Medicine than any of human kind.'

Homer, The Odyssey

Ancient Egyptian doctors were in great demand around the Mediterranean region. Rulers of other countries would often look to Egypt for a doctor when they were ill. So how did Ancient Egyptian medicine work?

Prevention

Doctors believed in prevention. They knew that good diet, rest and hygiene helped to prevent disease. Washing and keeping clean were very important, especially in such a hot country. They believed that keeping the gods happy was also a very important way to stay fit and healthy.

Treatment

Ancient Egyptians used natural ingredients such as berries, garlic, lotus flowers and honey in medicines. Lots of medicines also seemed to make use of animal manure. Many of these cures were based on careful observation of patients, and on trial and error.

Here is one example of a medicine used to stop people going bald: *'Fat of lion, fat of hippo, fat of cat, fat of crocodile, fat of **ibex**, fat of serpent, are mixed together and the head of the bald person is **anointed** with them.'*

And this medicine is designed to get rid of a headache: *'Flour, 1; incense, 1; wood of wa, 1; waneb plant, 1; mint, 1; horn of a stag, 1; sycamore seeds, 1; mason's plaster, 1; seeds of zart, 1; water, 1; mash, apply to the head.'*

Some doctors were very skilled at surgery and setting broken bones. Many excavated bodies show signs of broken bones having healed. Tools and scalpels were made from obsidian, a volcanic

An Egyptian doctor at work

rock that made a very sharp blade. Egyptian doctors knew a lot about how the body worked. For example, they knew that blood flowed through the heart. However, sometimes they got things wrong; for example, they believed people thought with the heart, not the brain! Many doctors learned their surgical skills working with the Egyptian army and dealing with soldiers who had been injured in war. They were also one of the first to

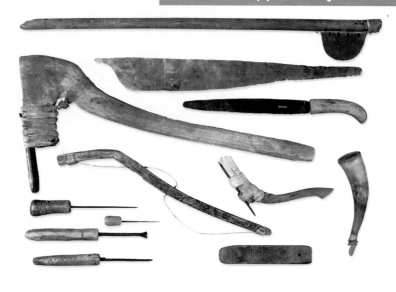

Ancient Egyptian medical tools, found in a tomb

develop anaesthetics, using crushed marble and vinegar, or sometimes opium, to deaden the pain and make operations easier.

Dentists could take out bad teeth and, if necessary, replace them with teeth made from bone.

Many of these cures and ideas were written down. For example, the Ebers Papyrus, which dates from around 1600 BCE, was found in a temple near Luxor and contains over 700 medical remedies and cures. It also offers advice on curing skin diseases, as well as hundreds of spells people should say to help keep them free from disease.

Think about it!

1. Which part of Ancient Egyptian medicine do you think is the most important – prevention or cure?
2. Do you think Ancient Egyptian medicine was 'more skilled than any of human kind'?

Let's do it!

1. How similar are the Egyptian medical tools to those in use today?
2. Research Ancient Egyptian surgery. How successful do you think it was?
3. Would you have been happy going to the doctor in Egypt 4000 years ago?

Key words

ibex

anointed

41

Just *how* inventive were the Ancient Egyptians? Making a convincing argument

Evil spirits

People believed they became ill when evil spirits 'invaded' the body, so religion had a part to play in preventing illness too. You could go to the temple of the god and pray for recovery. Special prayers were said over the sick person to help them get better, or sometimes over an **amulet**.

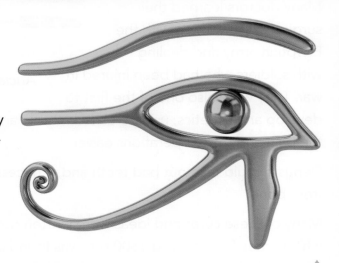

An amulet – such as the wadjet, or Eye of Horus – was said to keep evil away from anyone wearing it. Sailors often painted this symbol on the bow of their boats to keep them safe at sea

Amulets were worn to keep away evil spirits.

Think about it!

1. Why did Ancient Egyptians wear amulets?
2. Why might the special prayers work?
3. Which do you think was more important in Egyptian medicine – science or religion?

Wigs

In hot countries, it could be very difficult to keep hair clean and pest-free. So most Egyptians cut off their hair completely! They wore wigs instead. Ordinary people probably couldn't afford wigs, and you wouldn't want to wear a wig like this if you were working outside in the heat. But richer men and women wore wigs made from human hair, sometimes with sheep's wool and flax mixed in to give the wig 'body'. Sometimes, at parties, people would place a cone of incense on the top of their wig. This would slowly melt in the heat, letting out a nice smell and a cooling feeling.

Ancient Egyptian wig made from real hair

Let's do it!

Unit 7 asks the question, 'How inventive were the Ancient Egyptians?' Now it is time to answer that question for yourselves.

1. Split into two groups.

2. Group A will argue that they were very inventive. Work through Unit 7, and any other units in this book that might help, and produce a list of evidence that supports the idea that Egyptians were inventive.

3. Group B will argue that they were not very inventive. Work through Unit 7, and any other units in this book, and produce a list of evidence that supports the idea that Egyptians were not very inventive.

4. Once you have completed your list, put it in order. Rewrite it with the most important reasons at the top of the list and the least important reasons at the bottom.

5. Explain your list to the other group.

6. As a whole class, decide what is the 'best' answer to this question. Remember: you need evidence to support your conclusion!

Key word

amulet

43

8.1 Why is the rest of the world so fascinated by Ancient Egypt?

Discovery!

On 4 November 1922, Howard Carter found some steps leading down into tomb KV62 in the Valley of the Kings. It didn't seem to have been robbed. On 22 November, they made a small hole in the doorway and saw, by the light of a candle, what Carter described as 'wonderful things'. They had discovered the tomb of Tutankhamun.

Opening the tomb

It took several months to **catalogue** all they had found in the entrance to the tomb. It was February 1923 before they opened the sealed doorway that led into the main tomb. It was the most intact and best – preserved tomb yet discovered in the Valley of the Kings. And the world's press was on hand to record it. It took Carter 10 years to record everything that was inside the tomb.

▲ *Lord Carnarvon and Howard Carter in front of the tomb, November 1922*

Impact of the discovery

Howard Carter had been excavating in Egypt most of his adult life. Since 1913, he had been working for Lord Carnarvon. But KV62 made Carter's reputation. He toured Europe and America giving lectures to huge crowds. Suddenly, the world went 'Egypt-mad'. From popular music and films to building styles, from dresses to jewellery, the world became fascinated by Egypt. Tutankhamun became much more important in the 1920s and 1930s than he ever had when he was alive!

Tutankhamun's tomb was one of the few discovered in modern times that had not been robbed of its contents.

Egypt through history

This was not the first time the world had been fascinated by Ancient Egypt. Herodotus, the Ancient Greek historian, visited in 500 BCE and wrote about the building of the Great Pyramid at Giza. Napoleon, when he invaded Egypt in 1797, took scientists and archaeologists with him and they spent three years investigating visible remains. In 1799, some French soldiers discovered the Rosetta Stone in the Nile Delta. This had the same text written in three different languages, including Egyptian hieroglyphs and Ancient Greek. This made it possible for people to understand Egyptian writing.

Inside Tutankhamun's tomb; reconstructed for a travelling exhibition in the early 21st century

Throughout the 19th century, investigations in Egypt moved from treasure-hunting (many museums and rich individuals, like Lord Carnarvon, wanted mummies and artefacts to display) to serious research. By 1882, there was a British Egyptian Expedition Fund which paid for archaeological expeditions to Egypt. Some people, like Flinders Petrie – the first Professor of Egyptian Archaeology in London – spent much of their lives working in Egypt. Howard Carter had been one of Petrie's students.

Think about it!

1. Why do you think tomb KV62 made Howard Carter's reputation as an Egyptologist?

2. Why do you think discovering the tomb in 1922 had such an impact all around the world? (Clue: what had been happening in 1914–1918?)

3. Why was the Rosetta Stone such an important discovery?

The Rosetta Stone, now on display in the British Museum

Let's do it!

1. Research the tomb of Tutankhamun. Why were people so fascinated by the contents?

2. What happened to Lord Carnarvon after the discovery? Did this add to people's fascination with Ancient Egypt?

3. What happened to Howard Carter?

4. Which do you think was more important in helping us to understand Ancient Egypt – Tutankhamun's tomb or the Rosetta Stone?

Key word

catalogue

8.2 What do people find so fascinating about Ancient Egypt?

Skills and technology

Many people throughout history have admired the skills of the Egyptian pyramid-builders. The Great Pyramid of Giza, for example, was the tallest building in the world until the Middle Ages. Each side is around 230 metres long and less than 5 centimetres out of line, which is an amazing achievement of engineering. The Egyptians' architecture, temples and tombs have been widely copied throughout history. Egypt's craftsmen were very skilled. Their boats sailed around the known world. They traded widely with other countries. They even built a huge empire. Their ideas about medicine were adopted by the Greeks and the Romans.

The Louvre Pyramid, in Paris, was built in 1989

We probably feel as if we know the Egyptians better than any other ancient society. There is so much left behind.

Power and wealth

Egyptian rulers were immensely rich and powerful. Their stories fascinate us, as do those of strong and powerful rulers throughout history. Their unlimited power, and how they chose to use it, intrigues us and helps us to understand our own times. For example, how could a young king like Tutankhamun acquire so much treasure in such a short life? Remember that he was only 18 years old when he died!

Makeup was used by both men and women – for decoration and as protection from the sun

Culture and lifestyle

Paintings on the walls of tombs tell us about everyday life as well as the lives of the rich and powerful. Egyptians liked to party – music, dance and good food were very popular, just like today. And the country was rich enough for many people to enjoy these things.

Many of the problems faced by us today are similar to those faced by Egyptians all those centuries time ago.

The unknown

We are fascinated by new discoveries. Despite there being lots we do know about Ancient Egypt, there is still plenty we don't know. For example, what exactly was it that killed Tutankhamun? Or what happened to Nefertiti? She was there one day and then she just disappeared from the historical records. We don't even know where her tomb is. From time to time, there are new discoveries. For example, in December 2017, it was announced that two previously unknown tombs had been discovered near Luxor. They dated from around 1500 BCE. It is thought they were royal officials, but no one knows for sure who they were. And, in February 2018, the tomb of Hetpet was discovered. She was a priestess dating from around 2400 BCE. Female priests were quite rare at the time. This tomb contained very special paintings on the walls, including paintings of pet monkeys. All the time, new knowledge is being added to our understanding of Ancient Egypt.

Inside the tomb of Hetpet

Think about it!

1. Do you think that we are more fascinated by what we know about Ancient Egypt, or by what we don't know about it?

2. What do you think was the greatest achievement of the Ancient Egyptians? Why?

Let's do it!

1. Research one of the recent discoveries in Egypt (see above). What does it add to our understanding of Ancient Egypt?

2. Carry out a survey of people you know. Ask them what they know about Ancient Egypt, and what it is they find particularly fascinating.

3. Are their reasons the same as those given in this unit?

Should Egyptian artefacts go back to Egypt?

Museums and galleries

There are many museums and galleries throughout the world that display artefacts from Ancient Egypt. Over the last 200 years or so, archaeologists who have been excavating sites in Egypt have brought them back to their own country. Sometimes they have been bought – either legally or illegally – from grave-robbers or people who just happened to find something old and interesting. Some are also in private collections. Rich people seem to have a fascination with owning Ancient Egyptian artefacts!

Thousands of people visit these museums and galleries every year. This is not a surprise, seeing as the rest of the world is so fascinated by Ancient Egypt. It brings visitors and much-needed money to the museums.

In the last few years, important Egyptians have demanded more and more that items on display in museums around the world should be returned to Egypt and put on display there. This also applies to items owned by individuals. These Egyptians argue that many

Part of the Ancient Egypt gallery at the British Museum, London

of these items were stolen from Egypt before it ran its own affairs. They say these artefacts were taken by archaeologists like Lord Carnarvon in the 19th and early 20th centuries, or were bought from grave-robbers who had no right to dig them up and sell them. They say that all these items belong to the people of Egypt and no one else. If Egypt succeeds, what would happen to museum displays all over the world? Should all artefacts be returned to the country they came from originally?

Bust of Nefertiti on display in the ▶ Egyptian Museum in Berlin, Germany

Think about it!

1. Do you think Egypt should be able to take back artefacts on display around the world? Make a list of the arguments in favour of this idea. Make a list of the arguments against this idea. Which list is stronger?

Let's do it!

1. Hold a class debate with this title: 'The Rosetta Stone should be returned to a museum in Egypt.'

Skills grid

Unit	Skills
1	significance
2	chronology and sense of period, utility of evidence
3	using evidence to reach a conclusion
4	interpretations, similarity and difference
5	continuity and change
6	comparing the army of Egypt with that of another period
7	making a convincing argument
8	causation – why is the world so fascinated by Ancient Egypt?

Cape Town Is Running Out of Water

The South African city plans to shut off the taps to 4 million people. But it's just one of many cities around the world facing a future with too little water.
National Geographic, March 2018

▲ *Empty reservoir in Dubai*

Water

Everyone needs water – to drink, to wash, to grow food, to flush the toilet, to make electricity and for transport. However, many cities and countries today are running out of water, because of drought, population growth and increasing water use. Also, intensive agriculture is using more and more water.

Ancient civilisations

All early societies grew up around rivers – the Indus Valley, Sumer, the Shang in China, even Baghdad. Water for agriculture and transport was crucial to becoming rich enough for cities to grow. Many societies died out when the water supply failed. Many Maya cities, the greatest civilisation of Meso-America, disappeared following a drought from 820 CE to 940 CE. And, as we have seen in this book, Ancient Egypt was totally dependent on the flooding of the River Nile each year. No flood meant hunger for many people.

The city of Baghdad, founded in 762 CE, beside the River Tigris ▼

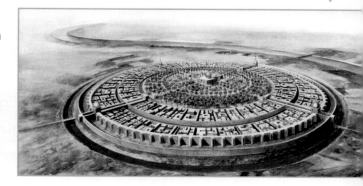

Writing a story

School curriculums emphasise the need to write fluently in a variety of styles, and to be able to communicate your ideas and emotions to others. History gives you the perfect opportunity to create a fictional story based on factual historical evidence you have discovered. Of course, you need to plan your story carefully before you start.

A river in Fiji that burst its banks, April 2012

You need to decide on:

- a setting – where your story is going to take place

- a main character

- a plot or structure to your story – what is going to happen, in what order

- history words you plan to use – these might include 'agriculture', 'farming', 'irrigation', 'shaduf', 'harvest', for example

- history facts or evidence you plan to include – if you based your story on the Nile and Egypt, you might include the three seasons, making sure the water reaches your field, and so on

- a conclusion – how your story is going to end.

Think about it!

1. Think about all the water you use every day. Do you have any idea how many litres of water you use? Or your family? Your school? What would life be like if you didn't have enough water? How would you have to change?

2. Where does your water come from?

Let's do it!

1. Write a short story based on the title 'The day the floods came', or perhaps 'The day the floods didn't come'. You could use the information you have learned from this book and set your story in Ancient Egypt, or you could set it in another historical period you know well. Remember to use facts and evidence from history to make your story realistic. Have fun!

Egyptian mummies

We have already seen (in Unit 5.1) how the Ancient Egyptians preserved their dead. They made them into mummies. They did this because they believed the dead person needed his body and internal organs in order to enjoy life in the next world. Of course, not all Egyptians were mummified. The poorer people were left to dry out in the heat and then buried.

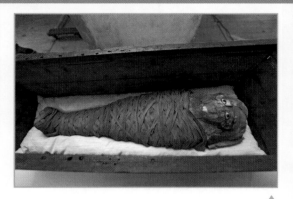

An Egyptian Mummy on display in a museum in Florida, USA

Mummies around the world

It wasn't just in Egypt that bodies were carefully preserved. The oldest mummies in the world, dating from around 5000 BCE, have been found in the deserts of Peru and Chile, in South America. It seems that these bodies were left exposed in the hot desert and became mummies naturally. The Aztecs, who ruled in Mexico from around 1300 until their defeat by the Spanish invaders, also mummified important people. However, these were often preserved in a sitting position, wrapped inside a woven bag and with their face covered by a ceremonial cloth.

There are lots of different ways to preserve a body!

Aztec mummy, dating from around 1400

Accidental preservation

Sometimes a body has been preserved by accident. Oti the Ice Man, for example, was found high in the Alps in the 1990s when a **glacier** began to melt. He had been attacked by others and left to die from blood loss and exposure. The ice had preserved him, which gives us a clear insight into life, clothes and equipment in Europe in around 3300 BCE.

Other bodies preserved by ice have been deliberate. For example, the so-called Siberian Ice Maiden dates from around 500 BCE and was carefully buried in a wooden coffin inside a mound. In her grave were goods from China, India, Iran and the

Mediterranean area. She was obviously very wealthy – a princess or a goddess – and had been very carefully buried.

In Bronze Age and Iron Age Europe men were sometimes sacrificed and then placed carefully into a peat bog. Tollund Man in Denmark is one example, but there are many more. The peat preserved their skin and skeleton. Often we can tell what their last meal was from the contents of their stomachs, and their skeleton tells us about their age and medical condition.

▲ *A modern woman on a horse, dressed up as the Siberian Ice Maiden*

Think about it!

1. How have each of these bodies been preserved? Have they been deliberately preserved, or were they preserved by accident?

2. Which conditions are best for mummifying a body?

3. If they knew how to preserve bodies, how inventive do you think these societies were?

4. What can we learn about the past from all these preserved bodies?

Let's do it!

1. There are plenty of other mummies around the world and throughout history. Find out if there are any near where you go to school. How similar, and how different, are they to those in this unit?

Key word

glacier

Egyptian hieroglyphs

There are over 1000 separate pictures used as hieroglyphs, each representing a sound. It must have been very difficult to learn to read and write in Ancient Egypt. We have already seen (in Unit 3.3) that very few Egyptians could read and write, so they paid a scribe to do their writing for them. This is not surprising, with so many symbols to remember. Hieroglyphs first appeared in Egypt around 3000 BCE.

Hieroglyphs carved into the wall of a temple, built around 2250 BCE

Each symbol represented a sound or word or object, so some symbols could mean more than one thing! Historians found it very difficult to understand hieroglyphs until the Rosetta Stone was discovered in 1799 (see Unit 8.1).

Other civilisations used their own forms of hieroglyphs too – the Maya in Meso-America and the Indus Valley Civilisation. We still can't read the Indus Valley script.

Ancient Sumer

Limestone tablet with picture writing on it, Ancient Sumer, around 3600 BCE. This may be the oldest writing in the world

Many historians believe writing first developed in Ancient Sumer. As a way to keep record of how many sacks of grain they were storing, people here used a sharp **stylus** to make marks on clay tablets.

Shang China

Around 1500 BCE, the Shang dynasty in China recorded events on turtle bones, which were used as **oracles** to predict events. Over 100,000 of these bones with writing on have now been discovered. Some seem to be prayers, but others describe events at the time. Later on, writing appears on bronze pots and pans too.

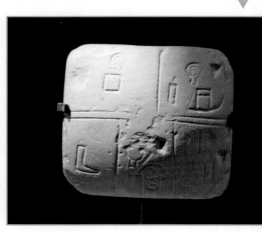

Ancient Greeks

The Ancient Greeks seem to have borrowed their alphabet from the Phoenicians, sometime around the 9th century BCE. Historians regard this as the first modern alphabet, written in a style we can easily recognise and read today. All modern forms of writing seem to have developed from it.

▲ *Early Greek alphabet on a cup*

What did people write on?

Sumerians wrote on clay tablets, Shang Chinese on bones, and Ancient Egyptians on papyrus. Paper was invented in China in around 100 BCE. However, it didn't spread to the Arab world until the 8th century CE, and it was 1100 before paper was used in Europe. In the 1440s, Gutenberg invented the printing press. Before that, each book had to be copied out by hand. In England, this was usually done by monks in monasteries. The printing press finally made printed materials cheaper and more widely available.

How did the invention of the printing press in the 15th century change reading and writing?

 Key words

stylus
oracle

Think about it!

1. Which of these examples would you classify as 'writing'?
2. Who, in your opinion, invented writing?
3. When was this?
4.. Why did people need to be able to write?

Let's do it!

1. Find out how to write your name in Egyptian hieroglyphs.
2. In your opinion, which was the most significant – the invention of writing or the invention of the printing press?
3. Do you think the written word has a future?

Ancient Egyptian gods

The Ancient Egyptians had a god for everything – over 2000 of them. Imagine how difficult it must have been trying to keep them all happy! There was a god to help you when you were going shopping, a god especially for scribes, a god to make you happy before you went travelling, and another one if you were travelling by river. The list seems to go on and on.

Ra the sun god

You can tell that Ra was important, because all the pharaohs were called 'son of Ra'.
When a pharaoh died, Egyptians believed that he rose into the sky and joined Ra. There are temples and pyramids dedicated to Ra all across Egypt.

Ra the sun god

Other important gods

Osiris was the god of the Underworld, the place where Ancient Egyptians believed people went after they died. It was important to be careful about upsetting him. Anubis was the god of embalming, Isis was the goddess whose job it was to protect the pharaoh, and Hathor was the goddess of love, music, fertility and beauty. Households often had their own little shrines to a god they found particularly important. It was widely believed that the gods intervened in a person's life (for good or for bad), so it was important to make offerings to them.

Think about it!

1. Why do you think the Egyptians had so many different gods?
2. How important do you think religion was in Ancient Egypt?

Around the world

Other societies had lots of gods too. The Maya worshipped hundreds of different gods, and so did the Greeks. The Romans adopted gods from all the countries they conquered. The Vikings and Anglo-Saxons had many gods before they became Christian, and the Arabs in the Arab peninsula had many gods before they became Muslims.

Similar beliefs

In Ancient Egypt, Ra the sun god travelled across the sky in his boat, from east to west. At the end of the day, he descended into the Underworld and sailed back to the east, ready to rise into the sky the next day. In Ancient Greece, Helios the sun god rode in his chariot across the sky, from east to west, then journeyed into the Underworld to start again from the East the next morning. In the Maya lands, the Jaguar god climbed into the sky in the

A sculpture of the Maya Jaguar God

east, and in the evening he descended in the Underworld, ready to rise the next morning in the east. Isn't it strange that three different societies use exactly the same story to explain day and night?

> *Why do you think these ancient civilisations had so many different gods?*

Helios, the Greek sun god

Let's do it!

1. Read the stories of the Jaguar god, Helios and Ra. Are they as similar as we suggest here?

2. Find out how other ancient societies explained day and night. Can you discover other stories similar to Ra, Helios and the Jaguar god?

3. Are the religious beliefs of Ancient Egypt similar to those of other societies you have studied? How?

Glossary

Adze: a carpenter's tool, like an axe, for shaping wood

Afterlife: the idea of life after a person has died

Amulet: bracelet or necklace designed to protect the wearer from evil or bad luck

Anointed: rubbed on

Archaeologists: people who study the past through discovering and excavating things left behind

Audiences: special meetings with people

Barter: to exchange goods without using money

Catalogue: to make a detailed list of

Cataracts: rapids; rocks that block a river, making it difficult to sail through

Criteria: rules for judging something

Delta: land built up by sediment from a river as it enters the sea

Excavated: carefully dug out of the ground

Feminist: demanding equal rights for men and women

Gender: sex – male or female

Glacier: a river of ice

Gruel: thin, watery soup or broth

Hieroglyphics: pictures or symbols used as writing

Ibex: a type of wild goat

Intensely: greatly

Irrigation: special canals to take water to the fields

Mercenaries: people from another country paid to fight in Egypt's army

Mistreated: treated badly, not treated correctly

Mummified: having dried up a body to preserve it

Necropolis: burial ground or cemetery

Niches: small spaces or alcoves

Oracles: gods or goddesses suggesting to people what they ought to do in the future

Papyrus: kind of thick paper, made from the papyrus plant, used for writing on before paper was invented

Predict: to tell in advance

Preserve: to stop bodies from rotting

Scrolls: rolls of papyrus, a kind of book in a long roll

Stylus: a sharp, pointed stick used for writing, like a pen

Utility: usefulness

Viziers: the most important person (after the pharaoh) who helped run the country; a 'prime' minister

Index

North Pole

GREENLAND

ICELAND

NORW

UNITED
KINGDOM DENM

IRELAND

GERM
A

FRANCE

PORTUGAL

SPAIN

MOROCCO

ALGERIA

CANADA

UNITED STATES
OF AMERICA

MEXICO

CUBA

JAMAICA

GUATEMALA

NICARAGUA

COSTA RICA

PANAMA

VENEZUELA

COLOMBIA

GUYANA

MAURITANIA

MALI

NIG

SENEGAL

GUINEA

NIGER

GHANA

ATLANTIC
OCEAN

Equator

ECUADOR

GABO

PERU

BRAZIL

PACIFIC
OCEAN

BOLIVIA

PARAGUAY

CHILE

URUGUAY

ARGENTINA

SOUTHERN

South Pole

ARCTIC OCEAN

RUSSIA

KAZAKHSTAN

MONGOLIA

JAPAN

PACIFIC OCEAN

...AINE

TURKEY

TURKMENISTAN

SYRIA

RAEL IRAQ

JORDAN

AFGHANISTAN

IRAN

CHINA

GYPT

SAUDI ARABIA

PAKISTAN

NEPAL

OMAN

INDIA

MYANMAR

UDAN

ERITREA YEMEN

THAILAND

VIETNAM

PHILIPPINES

SOUTH SUDAN

ETHIOPIA

SRI LANKA

...TIC ...GO

SOMALIA

KENYA

MALAYSIA

Equator

INDONESIA

PAPUA NEW GUINEA

INDIAN OCEAN

TANZANIA

SOLOMON ISLANDS

...BIA

MOZAMBIQUE

VANUATU

MADAGASCAR

A

AUSTRALIA

NEW ZEALAND

N

Acknowledgements

The publishers wish to thank the following for permission to reproduce images. Every effort has been made to trace copyright holders and to obtain their permission for the use of copyright materials. The publishers will gladly receive any information enabling them to rectify any error or omission at the first opportunity.

(t = top, c = centre, b = bottom, r = right, l = left)

p4t Lanmas/Alamy Stock Photo; p4b Khaled ElAdawy/Shutterstock; p6b Artokoloro Quint Lox Limited/Alamy Stock Photo; p7 Leemage/Contributor/Getty Images; p8 NASA; p9 robertharding/Alamy Stock Photo; p10 Arthit Kaeoratanapattama/Shutterstock; p11 age fotostock/Alamy Stock Photo; p12t Peter Hermes Furian/Shutterstock; p12b Jaroslav Moravcik/Shutterstock; p14 INTERFOTO/Alamy Stock Photo; p15 Ancient Art and Architecture/Alamy Stock Photo; p16 robertharding/Alamy Stock Photo; p17t robertharding/Alamy Stock Photo; p17b Heritage Image Partnership Ltd/Alamy Stock Photo; p18 BasPhoto/Shutterstock; p19t Chronicle/Alamy Stock Photo; p19b Heritage Image Partnership Ltd/Alamy Stock Photo; p21 Children play in a garden of a Middle Kingdom country estate (colour litho), Herget, Herbert M. (1885-1950)/National Geographic Image Collection/Bridgeman Images; p22t The Print Collector/Alamy Stock Photo; p22b Heritage Image Partnership Ltd/Alamy Stock Photo; p23 Granger Historical Picture Archive/Alamy Stock Photo; p24t © The Trustees of the British Museum. All rights reserved.; p24b DEA/A. JEMOLO/Contributor/Getty Images; p25 DEA/G. DAGLI ORTI/Contributor/Getty Images; p26 Egyptian scribe and Greek schoolboy (litho), English School, (20th century)/Private Collection / Look and Learn/Elgar Collection/Bridgeman Images; p28t Patchamol Jensatienwong/Shutterstock; p28b Carmen K. Sisson/Cloudybright/Alamy Stock Photo; p29 Paul Brown/Alamy Stock Photo; p31t WitR/Shutterstock; p31c Jakub Kyncl/Shutterstock; p31b BasPhoto/Shutterstock; p32 LUke1138/Getty Images; p33 Chronicle/Alamy Stock Photo; p36t Jim Henderson/Alamy Stock Photo; p36b Sergey Skryl/Alamy Stock Photo; p37 The Print Collector/Alamy Stock Photo; p38 Kazakova Maryia/Shutterstock; p39t Granger Historical Picture Archive/Alamy Stock Photo; p40 DE AGOSTINI PICTURE LIBRARY/Contributor/Getty Images; p41 © The Trustees of the British Museum. All rights reserved.; p42 valdis torms/Shutterstock; p43 © The Trustees of the British Museum. All rights reserved.; p44 Time Life Pictures/Contributor/Getty Images; p45t Petr Bonek/Alamy Stock Photo; p45b Reklamer/Shutterstock; p46t Viacheslav Lopatin/Shutterstock; p46b Christine Osborne Pictures/Alamy Stock Photo; p47 NurPhoto/Contributor/Getty Images; p48 Ian Dagnall/Alamy Stock Photo; p49 Vladimir Wrangel/Shutterstock; p50t Gretchen Mattison/Alamy Stock Photo; p50b JEAN SOUTIF/LOOK AT SCIENCES/SCIENCE PHOTO LIBRARY; p51 AFP / Stringer/Getty Images; p52t ZUMA Press Inc/Alamy Stock Photo; p52b Wikicommons; p53 Images & Stories/Alamy Stock Photo; p54t Leemage/Contributor/Getty Images; p54b World History Archive/Alamy Stock Photo; p55 National Archaeological Museum of Athens; p56 Vladimir Zadvinskii/Shutterstock; p57t Jorge Tutor/Alamy Stock Photo; p57b FALKENSTEINFOTO/Alamy Stock Photo.

We are grateful to the following for permission to reproduce copyright material:

An extract on page 20, *The teaching of Duaf's son Khety*, The British Museum, http://www.ancientegypt.co.uk/trade/story/main.html, copyright © The Trustees of the British Museum, 2019. Reproduced with permission; An extract on page 4 from *Travels in Asia and Africa 1325-1354* by Ibn Battúta, translated and edited by H. A. R Gibb, Routledge 2013, first published 1929. Reproduced by arrangement with Taylor & Francis Books UK; and an extract on page 23 from *Egyptian Women: Life in Ancient Egypt* by Caroline Seawright, copyright © 2001, http://www.thekeep.org/~kunoichi/kunoichi/themestream/women_egypt.html. Reproduced with kind permission.